ENDANGERED OCEAN ANIMALS

Dave Taylor

Crabtree Publishing Company

Endangered Animals Series

Text and photographs by Dave Taylor

To Don, who also thought I could do it

Editor-in-chief
Bobbie Kalman

Editors
Janine Schaub
David Schimpky

Cover mechanicals
Rose Campbell

Design and computer layout
Antoinette "Cookie" DeBiasi

Separations and film
EC Graphics Ltd.

Printer
Worzalla Publishing

Published by
Crabtree Publishing Company

350 Fifth Avenue
Suite 3308
New York
N.Y. 10118

360 York Road, RR4
Niagara-on-the-Lake
Ontario, Canada
L0S 1J0

73 Lime Walk
Headington
Oxford OX3 7AD
United Kingdom

Cataloguing in Publication Data
Taylor, Dave, 1948-
    Endangered ocean animals

(The endangered animals series)
Includes index.
ISBN 0-86505-533-5 (library bound) ISBN 0-86505-543-2 (pbk.)
Problems such as ocean pollution, oil spills, and hunting have caused marine mammals, birds, and fish to become endangered.

1. Marine fauna - Juvenile literature. 2. Endangered species - Juvenile literature. 3. Wildlife conservation - Juvenile literature. I. Title. II. Series: Taylor, Dave, 1948-   .
The endangered animals series.

QL122.2.T39 1993   j591.921   LC 93-30690

Contents

The world's oceans

Three-quarters of the earth is covered by oceans. The three large bodies of water that we call oceans are the Atlantic, Pacific, and Indian oceans. Oceans are important to all living things. They provide food and moisture for the earth and are instrumental in creating our weather. Ocean water evaporates, joins the water cycle, and becomes rain, fog, and snow.

Atmosphere helpers

Another important gift oceans give the earth is **algae**. Algae are tiny one-celled plants that play an essential role in slowing down **global warming**. Scientists believe that the earth is slowly growing warmer because gases, such as **carbon dioxide**, act like a blanket around the earth, preventing heat from escaping.

Absorbing carbon dioxide

Carbon dioxide is produced by car exhaust, industrial pollution, and forest fires. The removal of carbon dioxide from the air helps slow down the warming of the atmosphere. Trees change much carbon dioxide into oxygen, but ocean algae absorb more carbon dioxide than all the earth's rainforests combined!

Ocean pollution

Each year trillions of tons of sewage and dangerous industrial wastes are dumped into the oceans. Beaches are polluted by plastic litter and medical waste. Oil spills damage fragile ocean ecosystems. These harmful wastes kill thousands of species of fish, plants, and other marine creatures.

A threat to all life

Ocean pollution threatens everyone. Although many of us do not live near an ocean, the fish we eat, the air we breathe, and the temperature of our earth are all affected by ocean pollution. Isn't it time to protect the oceans of the world and the animals that live in it?

Animals in danger

In recent years people have forced many kinds of animals to struggle for survival. Hunting, farming, and the loss of wilderness areas have made life difficult and sometimes impossible for thousands of species of animals.

Terms of endangerment

Worldwide conservation groups use various terms to describe animals in distress. Animals that are **extinct** have not been seen in the wild for over 50 years. Animals referred to as **endangered** are likely to die out if their situation is not improved. **Threatened** animals are endangered in some areas where they live. Animals that are **vulnerable** may soon move into the endangered category if the causes that put them in danger are not corrected. **Rare** animals are species with small populations that may be at risk.

Endangered ocean animals

There is reason to be concerned about all ocean animals. Even if some species are not yet threatened or endangered, they may lose their lives because of pollution or commercial fishing.

There is hope, however. Due to the efforts of conservation groups, many animals that once faced extinction are surviving in healthy populations again.

Walruses can be found throughout the ice floes of the Canadian Arctic, Alaska, and northern Russia. They are endangered because of overhunting. These large relatives of the seal family were killed for their ivory tusks and for their blubber, which was made into oil.

The humpback whale

Whales are the largest animals on earth. They look like fish, but they are actually warm-blooded mammals. Whales nurse their babies and breathe air, as we do. Some whales even sing!

Many whales are now endangered. The humpback is one of these whales. There are fewer than 10,000 humpbacks left in the oceans of the world. Whaling has put them in danger of extinction.

Teeth or no teeth?

There are two families of whales: toothed and toothless. The humpback whale belongs to the toothless, or **baleen** family. Baleen are long, rough, hairy growths that hang down from the roof of the whale's mouth and help collect food. As the whale swims, the baleen act as a sieve, trapping huge amounts of krill, plankton, and tiny fish. Baleen whales grow much larger than toothed whales.

Underwater operas

Humpback whales are famous for their eerie songs. These songs can last as long as 30 minutes! Scientists have discovered that solitary males sing these songs in their winter breeding grounds, although they are not sure why. One theory is that these whales are singing to attract mates.

The sad story of whaling

The hunting of the humpback whale has been going on since prehistoric times. During the nineteenth century, the demand for whale products grew and so did the whaling industry.

Over two million whales were killed in commercial whale hunts! **Blubber**, which is the fatty material beneath the whale's skin, was boiled down into oil for lamps. Baleen was used to make many items, ranging from wagon springs to women's undergarments.

The killing continues

In 1966 laws were passed against the whaling of humpbacks. Under this protection, their population has slowly increased, but the killing of whales continues. Some countries have tried to get around the laws by saying they are involved only in "scientific whaling." They argue that they are catching whales to study them but, in fact, the whales are cut up and sold for profit. If humpback whales continue to be hunted, they may become extinct. It would be sad if the singing of these whales were lost to future generations!

Length: 57 feet (17.5 meters)
Weight: 10.5 tons (10,670 kilograms)
Where it lives: The Atlantic and north Pacific oceans

a humpback whale

(above) Humpback whales can hold their breath underwater for up to one hour. They breathe through blowholes, which are like nostrils at the top of their head. Their warm breath blows a cloud of vapor that can be seen from far away. (below) Scientists use photographs of the humpback's tail to identify individual animals. Each whale's tale is as unique as your fingerprints.

The Steller sea lion

The Steller sea lion is the largest of the **eared seals**, a family that includes sea lions and fur seals. Other seals are called **true seals**. There are two ways to tell these two families apart. 1. As their name suggests, eared seals have small ears, whereas true seals have ear openings. 2. Eared seals can walk on their four limbs and can even run if necessary. True seals cannot walk on land. Instead, they must "hump" their bodies across rocks and beaches.

Few sea lions left

The story of the Steller sea lion is a familiar one. Once, this marine mammal was found throughout the northern coasts of the Pacific Ocean, but in some areas its population is declining rapidly.

Hunted for their oil

In the early 1800s many Steller sea lions lived along the California coast. When settlers moved to California, they discovered that sea lion blubber could provide them with a ready source of oil. Before electrical lights were invented, great quantities of oil were needed for lamps. Between three and four sea lions were killed to make one barrel of oil. By the 1870s the sea lion population on the California coast was drastically reduced.

Shoot on sight!

Steller sea lions faced other problems as well. In 1899 the California Fisheries Commission announced that these seals were interfering with the state's fishing industry and should be shot on sight. One year later, another study revealed that sea lions had very little negative effect on the fishing industry. Unfortunately, this study did not change attitudes about Steller sea lions. People still believed that they were harmful. The killing of these sea lions continued into the 1930s, when a law was finally passed to protect them.

A continued decline

California's Steller sea lion population has dropped to fewer than 1000. Since these eared seals are now fully protected, the reason for their continued decline is not clear. Some scientists think that global warming may be responsible. As the temperature of the earth increases, the water in the southern parts of the sea lion's range may be growing too warm for this mammal and the fish it eats.

In Alaskan waters, the population of Steller sea lions has decreased by 82 percent. Between 1963 and 1972, 45,000 pups were killed for their coats. In 1990 all Steller sea lion populations were listed as threatened, but this has not helped these mammals. Fishing crews still kill sea lions when they come too close to a net.

Length: 11-12 feet (3.3-3.5 meters)
Weight: 600-2300 pounds (272-1043 kilograms)
Where it lives: The northern Pacific coasts

(opposite) In the late spring and summer male sea lions come ashore on isolated parts of the coast and claim a territory. When other males arrive, the first males must fight to keep the best spots and the right to breed with the females. Even after the young sea lions are born, the **rookeries,** *or breeding grounds, remain violent places. Angry males often toss newborn pups if they get in the way, and some pups are crushed as the males chase each other. (right) This sea lion looks more interested in sleeping than fighting!*

The brown pelican

There are seven species of pelicans in the world. All, except the brown pelican, like to live in freshwater lakes. This bird prefers the ocean, where it can feed off the fish that live there. The brown pelican is familiar to anyone who has vacationed on the beaches of the southern United States. The sight of this prehistoric-looking bird soaring over the ocean and diving from great heights is unforgettable.

A stunning dive!

Just before the pelican hits the water, its wings fold back and its neck shoots forward. Special air sacks on the pelican's chest cushion the bird as it comes into contact with the surface of the ocean. The blow of the diving bird stuns the fish. The pelican then uses its huge mouth like a net to scoop them up. The water drains out of its beak, and the fish remain.

Deadly DDT

Brown pelicans are an endangered species because of a chemical called DDT. This chemical was used to control insects in the 1950s. When DDT entered the ecosystem, it had a devastating effect on wildlife. Birds that ate insects built up harmful amounts of this chemical in their bodies and either died or could not reproduce.

Although brown pelicans do not eat insects, they were still affected by DDT. When waste from DDT factories was dumped into the oceans, small fish were poisoned by the chemical. As the pelicans ate the fish, they also ate the dangerous DDT. The eggs laid by female pelicans were weakened by this harmful chemical. The eggshells cracked upon being laid, and the baby pelicans inside died.

Greatly reduced populations

Before DDT was dumped into the oceans, 5000 pairs of brown pelicans were counted on one California island alone. That number was reduced to 100 in 1968 and then to 12 in 1969. By the 1970s the brown pelican had almost vanished from California, Texas, and Louisiana. In Florida the brown pelican had a different problem. In that state, developers destroyed pelican nesting sites to build houses, resorts, and condominiums.

Will this bird survive?

In 1972 the use of DDT was restricted by law. Even though the effects of the chemical have left the ecosystem, the brown pelican population has not yet recovered. Scientists believe that many of the fish that the brown pelican eats have been killed by the warming climate, which is a result of pollution. The future of this bird does not look promising!

Length: 48 inches (122 centimeters)
Wingspan: 84 inches (213 centimeters)
Where it lives: The tropical and subtropical coasts of the United States, Mexico, Central America, and South America

---

During their first year pelicans are brown. They turn greyish in their second year. By the time they are three, they take on adult colors.

Pelicans build their nests close together in trees or mangroves. In these nests the chicks hatch without feathers. They look like baby dinosaurs! The first chicks to hatch are the largest. They steal food from their younger brothers and sisters. Unless there is enough food for all the chicks, the largest are the only ones likely to survive to adulthood.

The harbor seal

Harbor seals live along northern coasts around the world. Unfortunately, these animals are decreasing in number. In some areas, they are already extinct. The decline in the harbor seal's number is due to oil spills, pollution of coastal areas, and the killing of seals by fishing crews who believe that the seals compete for fish.

True seals

Harbor seals belong to the family of true seals. Like all seals and sea lions, harbor seals find their food in the sea, but they must come to land to breed and give birth. They cannot walk on land as sea lions can. To move on land, they must "hump" themselves forward.

New pups

Once a year harbor seals shed their hair. This is called **molting**. Their breeding season begins soon after they molt. Males mate when they are six years old and females when they are three or four. Harbor seal pups are born on shore away from other seals. They usually weigh about 24 pounds (11 kilograms) and can swim almost immediately.

Covered with blubber

Harbor seals are covered by thick blubber and a thin layer of hair. The blubber allows these animals to live in very cold water. Although they possess this excellent insulator, harbor seals prefer to stay away from the ice floes of the north. They live farther south than any other seal except the monk seal.

Length: 4-5.5 feet (1.2-1.7 meters)
Weight: 550 pounds (250 kilograms)
Where it lives: The north Atlantic and Pacific coasts

In the water, harbor seals are quite agile. Their powerful hind flippers propel them with ease. On land, however, these seals cannot move as easily as their eared seal relatives can.

The California sea lion

The California sea lion lives in two separate areas of the world. One population is on the coast of California south to Baja, Mexico. It now numbers over 40,000 animals. The second population is in the Galapagos Islands off the coast of Ecuador. About 20,000 California sea lions live there.

California sea lions breed in June and July. After the breeding season is over, the males travel together and do not see the females or the pups for another year. When at sea, these sea lions leap like dolphins out of the water. When they rest, they float on the surface of the ocean in groups called **rafts**.

Where is my mom?

After giving birth on land, the female sea lions go back to sea to feed. If they cannot find their own pups when they return, the pups will die. No female will feed any pup other than its own. If one is bothered by a lost pup, she will grab it by the scruff of its neck and toss it away.

Brush with extinction

The story of the California sea lion's brush with extinction is similar in many ways to that of the Steller sea lion's. California sea lions were also targets of the seal hunters.

Although this sea lion is smaller than the Steller sea lion, it existed in greater numbers. California sea lions were easy to hunt because their rookeries were on California's mainland beaches.

Increasing in number

Today, the California sea lion population is much lower than it was 200 years ago, but it is increasing because of protection laws. The recovery of this sea lion shows that endangered animals can grow in number again!

Length: Female: up to 6 feet (1.8 meters) Male: 6.5-8 feet (2-2.5 meters)
Weight: Female: under 220 pounds (100 kilograms) Male: 600 pounds (272 kilograms)
Where it lives: The Pacific coast of North America and the Galapagos Islands

Male California sea lions bark constantly and can be heard from several miles away. They bark about three times a second. Females bark less than the males, but their bark has a wider vocal range.

Sharks

Shark! The very word strikes terror in the hearts of many people. Sharks have been the subject of books and movies, but the truth is not as scary. There are around 350 kinds of sharks, and only 30 types are known to attack people. There are fewer than 100 attacks reported each year, and less than 30 are fatal. Sharks don't actually eat people. They take a bite and spit it out. Scientists believe that sharks don't like the taste of human flesh. Of course, even a small bite from a shark can be deadly!

Looking for food

Sharks prefer to find their food among other ocean animals. Most sharks eat fish, although larger sharks prey on sea mammals. Some sharks bury themselves in the sand and lie there waiting for food to come along. Others prowl the open ocean hunting for a meal.

The smell of blood!

Sharks have nerve endings along their entire body. These nerve endings are called the **lateral line**. Sharks can feel unusual vibrations in the water with these nerves and can tell if the animal or fish making the vibrations is injured. Sharks also use their fine-tuned sense of smell and follow their noses to find prey. A shark can smell a single drop of blood in an area of ocean as large as a classroom. They also have good eyes. When sharks get close to their prey, they can see it even in the dark.

Jaws!

No one ever thought sharks would become endangered and need protection, but in the 1970s a book and movie popularized the hunting of sharks to the point that their population has dropped drastically. Why? Many people believe that sharks are dangerous. Statistics show, however, that millions more sharks are eaten by people than the other way around. Sharks should be the ones that are terrified!

Shark survival

Sharks swam the oceans over 350 million years ago, long before dinosaurs ever roamed the earth. They could survive for a long time to come, if human beings left them alone. As long as people continue to kill sharks for food and sport, sharks will continue to decrease in number. Some scientists fear that it may already be too late to save them.

Length: 6 inches-60 feet (15 centimeters-18 meters)
Where they live: In all the oceans of the world

(opposite top) The hammerhead shark's head resembles a hammer. Its nostrils and eyes are spread apart at either end of the head to allow this shark to track scents more efficiently. (bottom left) Most sharks have between four and six rows of teeth. Some have up to twenty rows. Sharks constantly lose their teeth when they feed. New teeth grow in to replace lost ones. A single shark may have over 10,000 teeth during its lifetime. (bottom right) The leopard shark is considered harmless to humans.

The elephant seal

There are two species of elephant seals in the world: the northern and the southern. The seas off Antarctica are home to the southern elephant seal, whereas the northern elephant seal lives along the Pacific coasts of Mexico and California. Both of these species were hunted for their blubber. The southern elephant seal survived years of hunting because it lived in remote and dangerous waters. The northern, however, almost vanished. Remarkably, its numbers have now recovered, and the elephant seal is out of danger.

The hunt for blubber

Like other members of this family, elephant seals have thick layers of blubber. Because of this blubber, the elephant seal was a favorite target of commercial seal hunters. By 1860 the elephant seal population was reduced to just a few animals. A herd of 400 found in 1880 was quickly killed. In 1890 a herd of between 20 and 100 animals was found on an isolated island. Of these, only a few survived.

A healthy population

For a long time no elephant seals were seen at all. Then, a few were found on islands where they were once plentiful. Gradually, the number grew. Today there are over 100,000 northern elephant seals living along the California coast. They are all the descendants of as few as ten animals!

Amazing discoveries!

Scientists have discovered some incredible facts about the elephant seal. In the 1980s experiments found that females can dive deeper than any other mammal. The deepest recorded dive by a female elephant seal is 4150 feet (1265 meters).

Dealing with pressure

At the depths to which the elephant seal dives, the pressure is so great that it would kill most mammals. Scientists are examining how the elephant seal is able to withstand this pressure. This research may help divers explore the deeper parts of the ocean.

Still holding my breath!

Scientists were even more amazed by how long elephant seals could stay underwater. These seals made two or three dives in an hour, spending only two or three minutes breathing on the surface between dives.

Length: Female: 6.5-10 feet (2-3 meters)
Male: 13-16 feet (4-5 meters)
Weight: Female: 2000 pounds (900 kilograms)
Male: 4400-5500 pounds (2000-2500 kilograms)
Where it lives: Pacific coasts of North America and South America; Antarctica

---

The elephant seal's nose resembles the trunk of an elephant. That is why it was given its name! There are now so many of these seals breeding along the coast of California that this area has become a favorite hunting ground of great white sharks. The sharks feed on elephant seals and other sea lions.

The manatee

At first glance, a manatee might remind you of a seal or walrus, but this mammal is not related to either. The manatee is a closer relative to the elephant than to the seal! Seals, sea lions, and walruses eat fish, clams, and octopuses, whereas manatees are plant eaters. Each manatee eats up to 30 pounds (13 kilograms) of aquatic plants each day!

Manatee species

There are three species of manatees, all of which live in warm coastal waters. The American species once lived throughout the waters of the southeastern United States, the Caribbean, and South America, but its population has dropped rapidly. It can no longer be found in many parts of its former range.

Unfortunate accidents

The manatee is endangered for two reasons: the pollution of coastal waters and motorboat accidents. Motorboats pass over the slow-swimming animals and cut them with the propellers. In winter, manatees like to move from the salty ocean water into the warm springs that feed freshwater rivers. Unfortunately, the risk of being hit by boaters is even greater there.

Slow movers

Manatees are slow-moving animals with few natural predators, apart from sharks and humans. Although they usually swim at about five miles per hour (eight kilometers), their speed may reach 15 miles per hour (24 kilometers) over short distances, if they are being chased.

Coming up for air

When moving from one feeding place to another, manatees come up for air every three or four minutes. When they are feeding, however, they stay underwater for nearly 15 minutes.

Mothers and their young

Between the ages of four and eight, female manatees are able to start breeding. They reproduce slowly, having one calf at a time. Unlike seals, manatees give birth in the water. Youngsters stay with their mothers one or two years.

Help for the manatee

The future of manatees is still in doubt, although numerous efforts are being made to help these mammals. New laws restricting the speed of boats in manatee areas have helped reduce the number killed. Sanctuaries have been created to protect manatees, and there are rescue units that capture injured ones and nurse them back to health.

> **Length**: 13 feet (4.5 meters)
> **Weight**: 500-2000 pounds (230-900 kilograms)
> **Where it lives**: Southeastern United States, Caribbean Sea, northern South America

The manatee is unique in many ways. No other large ocean mammal feeds on plants alone. Its only competitors for this food are sea turtles, but the competition is minor. Manatees basically have all the food to themselves.

Dolphins

There are more than 50 species of dolphins. The smallest is the Heaviside's dolphin, and the largest is the orca, or killer whale. All dolphins have teeth and belong to the family of **toothed whales**.

Dolphins live in all the world's oceans, and a few types can even be found in freshwater rivers such as the Amazon River in South America and the Indus River in Pakistan.

Echolocation

Dolphins navigate through the ocean by using **echolocation**. They produce a series of clicks that travel as soundwaves through the water. The soundwaves hit an object and reflect back, just as your voice echoes off a cave wall. The returning "echo" tells the dolphin the location, size, and shape of a fish. Dolphins also use echolocation to avoid enemies such as sharks.

Dangerous nets

The main reason dolphins are endangered is because of a fishing method developed in the 1950s. Fishing crews would spot dolphins feeding above a school of tuna fish, circle the school, drop their nets, and capture both the tuna and the dolphins. Sadly, the dolphins they hauled in were either drowned or crushed in the machinery before they could be released.

By 1972 nearly four million dolphins had been killed by this fishing method, and many injured dolphins escaped only to die later. In the 1970s laws were passed to stop this terrible practice, but they were not enforced. Dolphins continued to be killed in large numbers.

No tuna for lunch!

The future of the dolphin looked uncertain until a terrible event caught the attention of the world. In 1987 a tuna boat killed between 200 and 300 Costa Rican spinner dolphins, which made up half the population of this rare species! These terrible killings were filmed, and the film was shown on television.

It was discovered that during the 1980s 113,000 dolphins were killed in nets each year. Many people were so outraged that they stopped buying tuna. This forced tuna companies to use other methods of tuna fishing that don't hurt dolphins. Unfortunately, some fishing crews still use the old harmful methods.

Difficult to protect

Every dolphin population has declined in recent years. Even though a country can protect the dolphins living near its coast, little can be done to help the ones that are outside coastal waters. Protecting dolphins in these waters requires an agreement among several countries, which is very difficult to negotiate.

Other problems

Dolphins face other problems as well. Ocean pollution and decreasing numbers of fish are reducing their populations. Much is being done to save dolphins, but only time will tell if these efforts succeed.

> **Length**: 3.5-31 feet (1-9 meters)
> **Weight**: 88-9920 pounds (40-4500 kilograms)
> **Where they live**: Warm water ocean areas

Many people confuse the terms dolphin and porpoise. Although these two mammals are related, they look quite different. A porpoise (right) is smaller than a dolphin (opposite) and has a rounded snout. It has no beak, and its teeth are spade-shaped. A dolphin has more pointed teeth in both jaws. It has a rounded forehead, called a **melon,** *and possesses a beaklike snout.*

The southern sea otter

Sea otters are mammals that belong to the weasel family. They are the only members of this family that rely on the sea for all their food.

Shallow water

A sea otter's habitat is restricted by the depth of the ocean. Although sea otters can dive to a depth of 180 feet (55 meters), they prefer water that is not much deeper than 115 feet (35 meters). Female sea otters stay in shallower areas, whereas the males often head out to deeper seas.

Bloody noses

Female sea otters are easy to recognize because they have scarred or bloody noses. During mating season, the male sea otter bites the nose of the female and holds on tight. Males do this for two reasons. Biting prevents the female from escaping and keeps her near the surface of the water so both animals can breathe.

Sociable males

Male sea otters are more sociable than the females. Rafts of over 1000 males have been reported, and sightings of over 100 are common. A large female raft contains only about 20 females and their young.

Where have all the otters gone?

Once sea otters could be found on most north Pacific coasts. Today they are gone from most of that range, existing only in small isolated groups. The sea otter

half a million otters had been hunted and nearly three times that many were killed at sea and sank before trappers could recover the pelts. Sea otters were completely wiped out along the western coasts of Canada and California. A few survived in Alaska, but some hunting continued there.

A healthy comeback

In 1938 a group of fifty sea otters was found along the coast of California. Today this group numbers over 1500 animals. The more northerly sea otters number between 150,000 and 200,000. The sea otter has made a healthy comeback, although its future is still uncertain.

The danger of oil spills

Another great danger threatens sea otters—oil spills. When a sea otter gets oil on its fur, it cannot survive very long. The oil ruins the otter's coat, leaving the animal with no protection against the cold. The otter tries to lick the oil off and dies from this poison.

population has declined because this animal was hunted for its beautiful fur. In the nineteenth century, Russian explorers began trading for sea otter pelts with the native people that lived along the coast. The thick fur of the otter is so fine that it quickly became popular among fashionable people.

American and English fur traders also began hunting and trapping the otters. It wasn't long before these animals became rare. Unfortunately, this only made otter fur even more valuable! It looked as if the species would soon become extinct!

Almost extinct

In 1911 international laws were passed to protect the sea otter. By this time, over

---

Length: Female: 49 inches (125 centimeters)
Male: 53 inches (135 centimeters)
Weight: Female: 40-55 pounds (18-25 kilograms) Male: 33-100 pounds (15-45 kilograms)
Where it lives: Along the northern coasts of the Pacific Ocean

---

Sea otters spend most of their lives in the water. Sometimes they come out on dry land, but such visits are short. These jaunts are called **hauling out.** *Sea otters haul out only when they are sick or when the weather is very cold. Male sea otters do not migrate, but they often leave their areas of birth to search for females.*

Preserving ocean life

There are many ways you can help clean up our oceans and protect the animals that live there.

When you go to the beach, even if it is not at the ocean, make sure you do not litter. The garbage will eventually reach the sea, where it affects ocean ecosystems. You might even wish to bring a garbage bag to the beach and clean up the litter that careless people have left behind. You will be doing your part to preserve our oceans.

Be responsible

Make sure that when you or your parents use cleaners or other chemicals outside, that none is spilled on the ground. Every liquid that is dumped eventually ends up in the water. When your parents throw out chemicals such as motor-oil or paint, make sure these dangerous substances are disposed of properly.

Banning balloons

Most schools no longer release helium-filled balloons into the air during special occasions. These balloons ended up in the ocean, killing sharks and dolphins. If you see someone releasing balloons, inform them of the damage balloons can do!

Watching whales has become a popular pastime for tourists on the west coast of North America. Whale watchers go to special locations where these majestic animals swim. They can see whales splash their tail against the water's surface and blow vapor out of their blowhole. It is a thrilling experience to see these endangered animals in the wild!

Writing letters

One of the best ways to help ocean life is to write letters to the government. Encourage your government officials to stop the pollution of oceans. If people show that they care about preserving the ocean ecosystem, the government will also help protect it.

Thinking green

When you go to the grocery store with your parents, encourage them to buy green products. These products often cost more than regular products, but they help decrease waste and pollution. Buying these products shows that you support a healthy planet!

Glossary

algae Tiny plants that live in the ocean

baleen Long growths in the mouths of some whales that are used for collecting food

blowhole A breathing hole located on the top of the heads of whales and dolphins

blubber The layer of fat on some marine mammals such whales and seals

carbon dioxide A gas that is composed of oxygen and carbon and contributes to global warming

commercial Relating to a business or trade

conservation Protection from loss, harm, or waste, especially of natural resources such as wildlife

DDT A dangerous chemical used for controlling insects

echolocation The method used by dolphins and other toothed whales to locate objects in the water

ecosystem A community of living things that are connected to one another and to the surroundings in which they live

endanger To threaten with extinction

environment The setting and conditions in which a living being exists

extinct Not in existence; not seen in the wild for over 50 years

Galapagos Islands An island group located off the coast of Ecuador

global warming The theory that the earth is getting warmer because of pollution

groom To make neat and tidy in appearance

habitat The natural environment of a plant or animal

krill Small ocean animals with shells

mammal A warm-blooded animal that has a backbone and hair on its body

mangrove Tropical evergreen trees found in marshy areas

melon The rounded forehead of the dolphin

molt To shed feathers, skin, or hair in preparation for new growth

nurse To feed a baby with mother's milk

plankton Tiny plants and animals that drift in the sea

pollution Something that makes the environment impure or dirty

population The people or animals of an area; the total number of individuals living in a particular area

prey An animal that is hunted by another animal for food

raft A group of animals floating on the surface of the ocean

rainforest A dense forest in an area of heavy annual rainfall

range An area over which an animal roams and finds food

rare Uncommon; in serious danger of becoming extinct

reduce To make smaller

rookery A colony or breeding ground for seals or birds

sewage Human waste

species A group of related plants or animals that can produce young together

threatened Describing an animal that is endangered in some parts of its habitat

tropical Hot and humid; describing an area close to the equator

vulnerable Capable of becoming endangered

wean To make a young animal accustomed to eating food other than its mother's milk

Index

67 8 9 0 Printed in USA 1 0 9 8 7

DISCOVER SCIENCE
HEAT

Kim Taylor

Chrysalis Education

DISCOVER ● SCIENCE

Contents

US Publication copyright © 2003 Chrysalis Education
International copyright reserved in all countries.
No part of this book may be reproduced in any form
without written permission from the publisher.

Distributed in the United States by
Smart Apple Media
1980 Lookout Drive
North Mankato, Minnesota 56003

Copyright © Chrysalis Books PLC
Text © Kim Taylor Times Four Publishing Ltd
Photographs © Kim Taylor and Jane Burton
(except where credited elsewhere)

ISBN 1-93233-377-1
Library of Congress Control Number 2003102587

Designed by Tony Potter, Times Four Publishing Ltd

Illustrated by Peter Bull

Science adviser: Richard Oels, Warden Park School,
Cuckfield, Sussex

Origination by Bright Arts, Hong Kong

Typeset by Amber Graphics, Burgess Hill

Printed in Hong Kong

About this book

Why is the sun hot? What is really happening to wood when it burns? How do birds measure the heat of their eggs? Why does ice cream melt on a hot fruit pie? And what *is* heat, anyway?

In this book you can find out the answers to these, and many other fascinating questions. You can read about heat from the sun, and learn about the Earth's own heat that spills out in volcanoes and boiling pools. Find out how animals keep themselves warm, and how they cope in hot places. Discover also how important heat is in the modern world and how people have discovered many ways to create it for themselves.

Warning!
All experiments with heat can be dangerous. NEVER EXPERIMENT WITH MATCHES, FIRE, OR OTHER HOT THINGS UNLESS AN ADULT IS HELPING YOU.

What is heat?

Everything is made of tiny particles which are too small to see with the naked eye. When something is hot, its particles vibrate (move about). The hotter it is, the more the particles vibrate.

Heat is a kind of **energy**. It always passes from hot things to cold things, and never the other way. For example, if you put ice cream on a hot fruit pie, heat from the pie passes into the ice cream and melts it. The pie gets cooler and the icecream gets warmer.

The heat of the sun

Our sun is a star, a very hot ball of gas. Most of the heat on Earth comes from the energy that radiates from the sun. Without its heat, nothing on Earth could live.

Hot spots

The hottest parts of the Earth's surface are the areas of land where the sun's rays are most strong. During the day, these rocks in the Namib Desert in Africa are hot enough to cook an egg. Most desert animals spend the hottest part of the day in the shade.

Heat is produced when something is burned. In this bonfire, the burning wood combines with oxygen gas in the air to make heat. Flames are made by the burning gases that are given off by the wood as it is heated.

Hot hot hot!

Everything on Earth contains some heat. Even the particles in an iceberg are vibrating a little with heat energy. Although there is a minimum temperature (absolute zero, or minus 460°F) there is no known maximum temperature. The temperature at the center of the sun is about 25 million°F! But people can survive only when their body temperature is between about 80° and 104°F. Outside these limits it is either too cold or too hot and they soon die.

Burning gas produces heat. These extremely hot oxyacetylene flames are being used to cut through a great slab of steel. They reach 5900°F.

Electricity can produce heat. This electric spark is so hot it is being used to weld together pieces of steel. The spark reaches temperatures above 6500°F.

Did you know?

Death Valley, California, is one of the world's hottest places. Temperatures over 120°F (48°C) have been recorded there.

5

Making heat

Heat can be made in many different ways, each one using some kind of energy. An electric fire uses **electrical energy**, changing it into heat. A wood or coal fire uses **chemical energy**. We make body heat ourselves, using chemical energy stored in the food we eat. Huge amounts of **nuclear energy** are stored in some substances, such as uranium. This can be changed into heat in nuclear power stations.

The heat from a candle flame melts the wax of the candle, turning some of the wax into **vapor** (a gas). This gas, burning with oxygen in the air, produces heat and light. On page 11 you can find out what happens to a flame when no more oxygen is left.

Heat experiment

FACT OR FICTION?

You need
• A pen or pencil

1 Hold the pen or pencil firmly in one hand and rub it back and forth quickly on your sleeve, skirt, or pants.

2 After about 5 seconds of rubbing, hold the pen to your lips. Can you feel the part that has been rubbed?

3 Friction is the force that tries to stop things sliding over each other. Energy is needed to overcome this force, and the energy is turned into heat.

1

2

3

4   5

Crystallizing heat

When a liquid forms **crystals**, it gives off heat. Here you can see the inside of a handwarmer (1), a device to help people keep warm in cold places. It contains a special liquid. When the red plastic rod is bent (2), crystals start to form and spread right through until the liquid is all crystallized (5). This makes the bag warm to hold.

Burning heat

Like the candle flame, this flame is made by mixing gases. Here gas from an oil well is being burned with oxygen in the air.

Friction heat

Heat can be produced by rubbing things together. This is because of a force called **friction**. This fast car's tires spinning against the road surface are hot because of friction.

Human heat

Hard physical work makes you feel hot. This is because your muscles turn energy from your food into heat energy as well as movement. This sportsman is hot because he has been running fast. People's bodies sweat to cool down (see page 20).

Electricity is a form of energy. When it is made to pass through a thin wire, as in this electric fire, some of it is turned into heat. The wire glows with heat and helps to warm up a room.

Did you know?

Birds burn up food fast to provide energy for flying, so their body temperatures are usually higher than mammals'. Sparrows, for example, are 7°F warmer than people!

Measuring heat

Heat can be measured in two different ways: as temperature (hotness) or as the amount of heat energy something contains (see page 9). Thermometers are instruments that are used to measure temperature. Some are marked with measurements in degrees Celsius (°C). Water freezes at 0°C and boils at 100°C. Some thermometers are marked in degrees Fahrenheit (°F). Water freezes at 32°F and boils at 212°F.

This baby chicken is just hatching out. An egg has to be kept at an exact temperature in order to hatch. A mother hen can judge the temperature of her eggs to within half a degree. She uses a bare patch of skin on her chest, called the brood patch.

Did you know?

The ancient Egyptians hatched chicken's eggs in mud huts heated by fires. They judged the heat of the eggs by holding them against their cheeks.

Heat experiment

HOT LIPS

You need
• Two mugs
• Two teaspoons
• Thermometer
• Warm and cold water

1 Fill both mugs with a mixture of warm and cold water. Put slightly more warm water in one mug than the other.

2 Take the temperature of each mug of water, adding small amounts of warm or cold water until one is about 9°F warmer than the other.

3 Put a teaspoon in each mug and leave them there for at least half a minute. Take the spoons out in turn and hold each for a second against the tip of your finger. Can you tell which is the warmer spoon?

4 Put the spoons back in the water for half a minute. Then test them against the back of your hand. Repeat, testing the spoons against your lips. Which can judge differences in temperature best, fingers, hands or lips?

There thermometers measure temperature in various ways.

This medical thermometer contains a thin tube filled with mercury, a liquid metal. Mercury expands and rises up the tube when it heats up.

This thermometer contains alcohol (colored blue). When it is heated, the alcohol expands and rises inside the glass tube.

This is an aquarium thermometer. It contains special dyes that change color as they are heated. The green window shows the temperature of the water in the aquarium.

8

Each color on this chart represents a temperature. The chart is used to measure the temperature of hot metal.

1280°C
1200°C
1100°C
1000°C
900°C
800°C
700°C
600°C

Color temperature

The steel bar on the left is at about 1100°C. The color chart (above) can be used to judge the temperature of hot metal. That is because metal changes color as it is heated. It starts to glow red when it reaches 1112°F. As it gets hotter, its color changes to orange and then to yellow. Finally, it becomes white hot.

Heat energy

Temperature and heat energy are not the same thing. If you add a teaspoon of very hot water to a bowl of cold water, it will not make much difference to the temperature of the water in the bowl. However, if you add a glassful of warm water, this *will* make a difference because the water in the glass contains more heat. The water in the glass is at a lower *temperature* than the water in the spoon, but it contains more *heat* energy.

Fire

When something burns, it combines with oxygen in the air. Heat and gas are produced. You can see and feel the heat. The gas is clear, so you cannot see it. Smoke is often formed, too. It is made of tiny particles that have not burned completely.

1 Dry leaves and twigs contain a lot of **carbon**. Fire spreads through them quickly.

2 Heat from burning twigs turns part of the other twigs into gas, which burns as a sheet of flame.

3 When the gas is all burned the bigger branches have been turned into **charcoal**, which is almost pure carbon. It glows red hot.

4 All that is left is soft powdery **ash**. It consists of chemicals in the wood that will not burn.

Firefighting

Gasoline is very dangerous because it lights easily. But even gasoline fires can only burn if they are supplied with oxygen. Thick foam from a fire hose stops oxygen getting to the surface of the gas and the fire is put out.

Did you know?

It is thought that people first learned to make fire for themselves about 450,000 years ago.

Heat experiment

FLINT AND STEEL

You could also try this with a lighter flint and a nail file.

You need
• A lump of flint from a road or beach
• A file

1 In a dimly-lit or dark room try striking the flint against the file. Make the flint slide a bit over the rough surface of the file. With practice, you should be able to produce sparks.

In the first picture (above left) you can see a lighted candle floating on water, with a glass jar over it. As the flame burns, it uses up the oxygen in the jar. On the right, you can see the same candle a short time afterwards. Water has been sucked in to replace the oxygen, making the water level rise. All the oxygen in the jar has been used up, so the flame has gone out.

Friction of flint on steel produces so much heat in one spot that bits of fire are heated red-hot and fly off as sparks. People used flints to light fires before matches were invented.

Solar heat

Heat travels from the sun through space as **electromagnetic waves**. By the time these waves reach Earth, they have spread out and are not burning hot. Nearer the sun, the planet Venus is extremely hot all the time. Further from the sun, Mars is too cold for life.

Did you know?

It takes eight minutes for radiant heat and light from the sun to travel the 92 million miles to Earth.

Plant leaves, like this oak leaf, collect heat and light from the sun. They use light energy to make plant food from carbon dioxide gas in the air. Heat from the sun warms the leaves to speed their growth.

Energy from the sun

The sun is a star, a glowing ball of very hot gas. Its heat comes from deep inside, where atoms of hydrogen gas crash. As they come together, energy is released.

The sun's heat warms the Earth and produces the weather. This makes currents of air move and causes winds and rainfall. You can find out more about this on pages 24–25.

When the sun's rays pass through a lens, they can be focussed onto a small spot that becomes very bright and very hot. Here a lens is focussing light onto a dead leaf, which is beginning to smoke as the sun's rays heat it up.

Dark objects absorb more heat than light-colored ones. These rocks in a desert in Africa are almost black. They absorb heat from the sun during the day and become too hot to touch. Even so, some orange lichens can grow on them.

Solar flare

The sun's surface temperature is about 10,000°F. The temperature inside is far greater (see page 5). Here you can see a huge solar flare, an explosion on the surface throwing particles far out into space.

The sun's heat is very important to cold-blooded animals because it provides them with warmth (see pages 18–19). This dragonfly is drying its damp wings and warming its body so that it can fly.

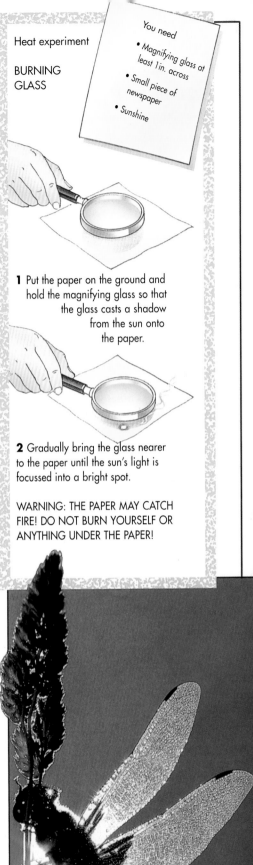

Earth heat

The center of the Earth, its core, is very hot. Some of the core is liquid white-hot iron at 3632°F. Nearer the surface, there is red-hot liquid rock called magma. Magma sometimes flows up to the surface where there are cracks in the Earth's crust. It then flows out as lava.

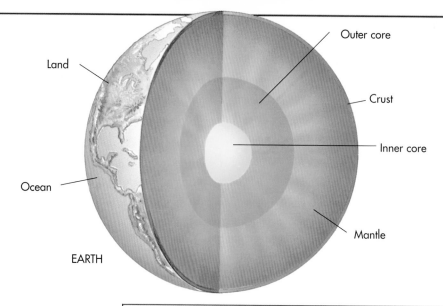

Land

Ocean

EARTH

Outer core

Crust

Inner core

Mantle

Did you know?

Deep mines become so hot due to Earth heat that miners would roast if there were no air-conditioning.

Volcanoes

Volcanoes are formed when there is a crack in the Earth's surface. Red-hot magma shoots out from the inside of the Earth when a volcano erupts, as this one is doing in Hawaii. It forms a glowing hot river of lava. Even during the day (below), you can see the lava flowing down the mountain.

Heat from inside the Earth can also seep to the surface and cause mud pools to boil. This happens where the Earth's crust is thin. As the mud bubbles burst they form strange shapes. There are famous boiling mud pools in Iceland and New Zealand.

Earth power

Where the Earth's crust is thin, it is possible to build power stations to use the heat energy below the ground.

This power station in New Zealand uses the Earth's natural heat to produce power to heat and light homes.

In places where the Earth's inner heat is near the surface, rocks and water heat up. Sometimes steam comes spurting out of the ground in a **geyser**. Some geysers spurt all the time, while others spurt only from time to time. This geyser is squirting up through a pool of water, so the steam carries water up into the air with it.

Heat experiment

SODA GEYSER

You need

- Small, wide-mouthed bottle or jar with a plastic lid
- Drinking straw
- Sticky tape
- Vinegar
- Sodium bicarbonate

1 Ask an adult to make a hole in the lid of the bottle so the straw fits tightly.

2 Push the straw in so its end is about 1in. above the bottom of the bottle. Fix it firmly to the lid with sticky tape.

3 Fill the bottle three-quarters full with cold water and add 1–2 tablespoons of vinegar.

NOW PUT THE BOTTLE IN THE KITCHEN SINK OR DO THE REST OF THE EXPERIMENT OUTDOORS!

4 Put a teaspoon of sodium bicarbonate into the bottle, while a friend quickly puts on the lid.

Acid in the vinegar acts on the sodium bicarbonate to make carbon dioxide gas. This causes water and bubbles to squirt out like a geyser.

Plant warmth

In order to grow, plants need warmth, which they get from the sun. Very few plants can make their own warmth. However, plant material can be turned into warmth by **bacteria** and **fungi**. They can rot a pile of dead leaves, making it warm-up and even start to steam. In fact, if hay is stacked when it is too green and fresh it can heat up so much that it catches fire!

Snake hatch

Female garter snakes often lay their eggs in a heap of dead leaves. As the leaves rot they heat up, gently warming the eggs. The young snakes cut slits in the soft egg shells and look out as they hatch.

> **Did you know?**
>
> An Australian bird, the Mallee Fowl, builds a pile of leaves which rot, making enough heat to hatch its eggs. The bird adjusts the temperature by adding or removing leaves.

Plants in hot places

Cactus plants are mostly found in hot climates. This candelabra cactus is well equipped to withstand the extreme heat and dryness of the Mexican desert. Its swollen stems contain a supply of water. The stems absorb heat and become warm during the day.

Heat experiment

COMPOST

1 Collect fresh grass cuttings from a park, yard or playground. Pack the cuttings into the polyethyene bag.

2 Put the bag into the insulated container and leave it overnight.

3 Next morning, measure the temperature of the air outside the box. Then put the thermometer right into the middle of the bag of grass. Compare the two temperatures.

4 Record the temperature of the compost each morning for a few days. Does it rise or fall?

M	T	W	Th	F	S	Su
72	74	76				

Bacteria and fungi start to work as soon as grass is cut. They break down the grass, making carbon dioxide gas and heat.

The temperature inside a heap of rotting plant material rises as bacteria and fungi get to work. The middle of the heap can become too hot for animals to live. Worms live in the part that is just the right heat for them.

The arum (below) is one of the few plants that make heat. When the flower first opens the spadix (the tall, pointed brown piece in the middle) is warm to touch. The warmth helps to attract small insects that fall into the flower and are trapped. They are later released, covered in pollen.

When dead leaves sink to the bottom of a pond they rot and give off heat and gas. The gas bubbles up to the surface. It may be **methane**, which will burn with a blue flame if you light it.

Warming up

People and animals make heat in their bodies. The heat comes from the food they eat when it combines with oxygen in the body **cells**. This process is like burning (see pages 10–11) but is slower. The food is burned to make heat and muscle power. Warm-blooded animals make heat all the time, even when they are still. Cold-blooded animals can make heat only when they move. The more active an animal is, the more heat it makes.

This tiger moth is at rest on a flower.

Now it buzzes its wings, ready for take-off.

Shivering snakes!

Snakes are cold-blooded animals so they can make their own heat only when they move about. But a mother python has to keep her eggs warm so that they will hatch. She does this by curling her body around the eggs and shivering to make heat. This baby python has just hatched. It is very fierce.

Moth sloth

Some moths, and some other insects, cannot fly at all until their bodies have warmed up. The tiger moth (see above) is unable to take off even when danger threatens. It first has to buzz its wings for half a minute or so. Buzzing works the wing muscles, making enough heat to warm the body. Then the moth is able to fly.

18

Hot dogs

Warm-blooded animals, like these dogs, make a lot of heat when they run. Blood carries oxygen and food energy to the muscles. The muscles work the legs back and forth, so they move and produce heat.

Heat experiment

BODY HEAT

You need
• A medical thermometer
• An adult to help

1 Ask the adult to take your temperature on a cool day when you are feeling cold and shivery.

2 Do the same thing after you have been running about a lot and are hot and sweat. Is your temperature different?

Mammals, including people, can regulate their body temperature to within a fraction of a degree, regardless of whether the outside temperature is hot or cold.

Some cold-blooded animals, like this chameleon, warm up their bodies by basking in the sun until they are really hot. A nicely warmed-up lizard or chameleon can act quickly when in danger, but a cold one is sluggish and may get caught.

Did you know?

Rattlesnakes have heat sensors on their heads so sensitive that they can detect the body of an animal nearby even if it is less than 2°F warmer than its surroundings.

Cooling down

Too much heat can be a problem. Small animals can hide underground during the day. Larger animals find a cool place to sit or stand. Animals can also make their bodies lose heat. Elephants, rabbits, and the fennec fox (see the opposite page) lose heat through their large ears. Humans lose heat by sweating.

A black dog gets hotter in the sun than a brown dog because black absorbs more heat. So the black dog has to lie in the shade to keep cool.

Running shower

When your body is hot, water or sweat **evaporating** from the skin takes heat from your body and cools you down. A shower from a bottle is very cooling, as this runner knows.

asics

ADT

ADT
London
Marathon
92

1002

UNISYS

20

Did you know?

Many mammals, birds, and some reptiles cool down by panting. This allows water to evaporate from the mouth and lungs.

Hippos keep cool by spending the day in the water. The river water flowing past their bodies cools them down. At night they come out to feed.

This fennec (a desert fox) is well-adapted to life in the African desert. Its enormous ears give it a large area from which it can lose heat, and so keep cool.

In hot places where there is little shade, people tend to wear *more* clothes, not fewer, to keep themselves cool. This man belongs to the Tuareg people of the Sahara Desert. The long, flowing robes protect him from the sun's heat.

Keeping cool

These houses are cool inside because they have small windows which do not let in much sunshine, and the walls are painted white. White reflects the sun's heat back into the sky.

Heat experiment

ON REFLECTION ...

You need
- Black card
- White card
- Scissors
- Electric lamp

1 Cut out a rectangular piece of black card about 1in. X 1.5in. Cut out another from white card, the same size.

2 Make a fold 0.5in. from the end of each piece of card. Open out the folds at right angles.

3 Pick both cards up by the right-angled pieces and hold them so they are about 2in. away from the heat of an electric light. Keep them there for at least 5 seconds. Now feel them with your lips. Which card is warmer? Why do you think this is?

Moving heat

Heat energy always moves from hot things to cold things, but it can do so in various ways. It can travel through some materials such as metal quite easily. This is called **conduction**. Heat can move by **radiation**, traveling in rays through air and space at the speed of light. Heat can also move in currents of warm air or water. This is called **convection**. A hot drink in a cup loses heat by all three methods—by conduction into a spoon or the table on which it sits, by radiation into the room where it is absorbed by the walls, and by convection into the air.

Conduction experiment

Four rods made of different materials are coated with wax and stuck into a block of metal. The metal block is then heated with a gas burner and heat from it is conducted along the rods. The aluminum rod (bottom) conducts heat best, so the wax has almost melted away. The next rod up is brass, then steel, then glass. Glass conducts very little heat, so the wax on this rod has not melted.

Did you know?

Silver conducts heat so well that a solid silver teaspoon in a hot drink becomes too hot to hold.

Animal warmth

Heat from the body of this bird sitting on her nest passes into her eggs to keep them warm. This is essential if her eggs are to hatch out successfully.

You need
- Copper wire
- Steel wire
- Pliers
- A mug
- 8 pins
- Vaseline
- Hot water
- Newspaper

1 Cut one 6in. piece of copper wire and another, the same length, of steel wire.

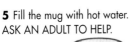

2 Use pliers to bend each wire at right angles, 2.5in. from one end. Bend the shorter arms back on themselves about 0.75in. from the right angle.

3 Hang the bent wires on the edge of the mug. Stand the mug on newspaper.

4 Smear the tops of the pins with vaseline and stick them along the wires.

5 Fill the mug with hot water. ASK AN ADULT TO HELP.

6 Watch what happens. Heat is conducted along the wires and melts the vaseline, causing the pins to fall. Which pins drop off first. Which wire conducts heat quicker?

Hot black

Heat from the sun is absorbed by black rocks, so they get very hot. If you put your hand on one of these rocks during the day, you would find it felt hotter than the light-colored rocks around it. The paler rocks reflect the heat and so stay cooler.

Still air conducts very little heat away. Soft fur, like that on this rat, traps still air and keeps the animal warm. However, water conducts heat away and uses heat when it evaporates, so an animal with wet fur will soon feel cold. It is important for this small animal to dry its fur quickly, or it will get chilled.

Waste heat

An open fire is very wasteful of heat energy. Three-quarters of the heat goes up the chimney by convection. Only one-quarter warms the room by radiation.

Hot air

As air is heated, it expands and rises. Air over land heats up more quickly than air over the sea. As the warm overland air rises, cool air rushes in off the sea to take its place.

That is why on sunny days there is nearly always a sea breeze by the coast. In this picture, clouds have formed from the warm air rising just above a small island.

Shimmering heat

Hot air is less dense than cold air. When the two meet and mix you can often see a shimmering effect. This is because light is bent when it passes from one density to another.

Air burn

Really hot air looks the same as cold air, so you have to be careful when using a blower to strip paint. Coils of wire made red-hot by electricity heat-up the air inside the blower so that it comes out hot enough to melt paint.

24

Clouds, wind and rain

The sun's heat drives the Earth's weather, making winds blow, clouds gather, and rain fall. Clouds form when warm, damp air rises into cooler air. The water vapor in the warm air **condenses** into tiny droplets, forming a cloud. If the cloud goes on rising, more water condenses and the droplets get bigger. Then they start to fall as rain.

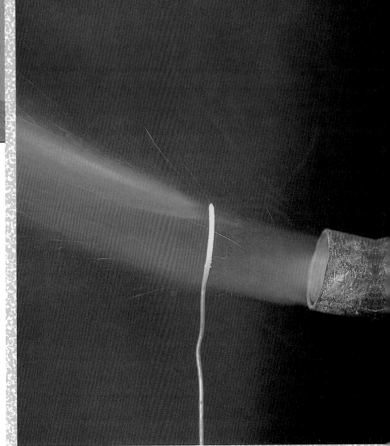

The flame from a gas blowtorch is mostly very hot air. Gas burns with a blue flame when it has plenty of oxygen. If it is starved of oxygen, the flame turns yellow and sooty.

Heat experiment

UP UP AND AWAY

You need
• Tissue paper
• Scissors
• An old plate
• Matches

ASK AN ADULT TO HELP YOU.
DO NOT USE MATCHES ON YOUR OWN.

1 Cut out a piece of tissue paper about 4in X 8in. Curl it round to make a tube.

2 Stand the tube on a plate. Light the top of the tube with a match. Watch what happens!

As the flame burns down the paper, it makes a rising column of hot air above it. When the paper is all turned to ash, it is then so light that it gets sucked up into the rising warm air.

Storing heat

It is not easy to store heat, because it is always trying to escape. It eventually escapes even through thick layers of **insulation**. But other forms of energy can be stored and later turned into heat. Food is a source of energy, so a food store can be a heat store. Animals store food in their bodies as fat. Fat is not only a good insulator, but can also be turned into body heat.

Heat experiment

SOME KEEP IT HOT!

You need
- Two small jars with lids
- One large jar with a lid
- Newspaper
- A wide-mouthed Thermos bottle
- Ice cubes

1 Tear up enough pieces of newspaper to make an insulating layer in the big jar.

2 Put equal numbers of ice cubes in the two small jars and the Thermos bottle. Screw the lids on tightly.

3 Put one small jar inside the large jar and quickly pack the newspaper all around it. Screw the lid on the big jar.

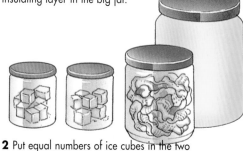

4 Wait until the ice in the jar you can see is melted. Unpack the other jar. Are the ice cubes in it still frozen? How much ice is there in the Thermos bottle?

The newspaper is a good insulator. It keeps heat from the ice.

Hot bottle

A Thermos bottle slows down the escape of heat. The inner container is made of two layers of silvered glass separated by a **vacuum**. As there is no air in a vacuum, heat does not escape across the gap. A little heat is lost by radiation from the silvery glass and more escapes through the top, but a drink can stay hot inside for hours.

This machine is digging coal out of the ground. **Fossil fuels** (coal, oil, and gas) are all the remains of plants and animals that lived millions of years ago. They collected energy from the sun and that energy is still there. When we use these fuels, we release the stored energy as heat.

Body warmth

Warm-blooded sea animals need to be well insulated so that their body heat does not escape into the cold water. They have a layer of fat, called **blubber**, under the skin to keep the heat inside. This baby seal is warm inside a furry coat with its lining of blubber.

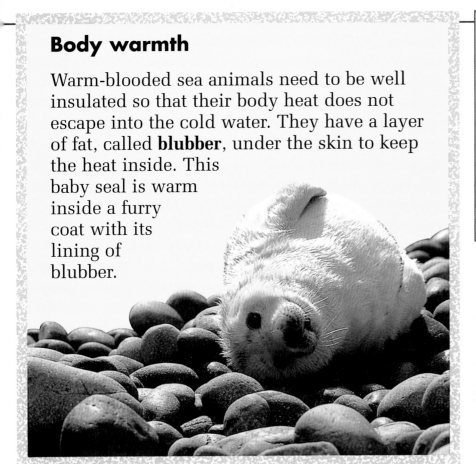

Did you know?

The Thermos bottle was invented by Edward Dewar in about 1895. It was first used to keep liquid gases cold, not to keep things hot.

Heat trap

The silvery plastic sheeting around this tired marathon runner reflects heat from his body back towards him. It stops him getting chilly after the race.

This hornet is having a quick meal of sugar water. The sugar will be converted into energy so that the hornet can buzz its wings and fly. It has to feed often because it can store very little energy.

Food stores

Some small animals, like this mouse, store food for winter. The mouse is able to keep warm in the cold weather by eating its food store.

The effects of heat

Heat makes some things expand, which means they get bigger. A metal rod is slightly longer when it is hot than when it is cold. The amount of expansion depends on the kind of metal. Heat also makes solids melt and liquids boil.

Mud crackers

Heat dries things out by evaporating the water they contain. The sun's heat dried up this mud. The mud shrank as it dried, leaving a pattern of cracks. If you imagine water poured into the cracks, you can get an idea of how much water it once contained.

Spread your wings

Birds that dive for fish, as this cormorant does, cannot fly when their wing feathers are soaked. They spread out their wings and dry themselves in the sun so they can fly again.

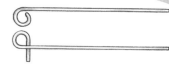

You need
- Two paper clips
- Two pins
- Two blocks of wood
- A candle
- Fine pliers

Heat experiment

EXPANDING METAL

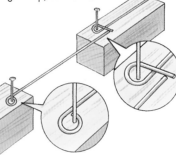

1 Use the pliers to straighten the paper clips. One will be your expander and the other will be your pointer. Bend one end of each into a small loop to fit the pins. Give the pointer a longer loop, as shown.

2 Pin the pointer on one block of wood and the expander on the other so the end of the expander rests against the loop of the pointer.

3 Carefully move the blocks together until the pointer starts to move.

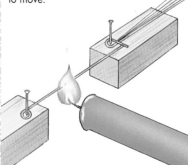

4 Light the candle and use it to heat the expander. Watch the tip of the pointer.

Heat causes the expander to expand and push against the loop of the pointer. The pointer is a sensitive lever, so a tiny movement at the loop end makes the tip of the pointer move much more.

Because metal expands when it heats up, railroad lines used to have gaps in them at regular intervals. This allowed the rails to expand in hot weather without buckling the rail and causing an accident. Modern rails are treated in a special way so there is very little expansion. This gives rail passengers a smoother and quieter ride.

Did you know?

The eggs of some reptiles (particularly turtle and alligators) can develop into either males or females depending on the temperature at which they are kept.

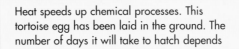

Heat speeds up chemical processes. This tortoise egg has been laid in the ground. The number of days it will take to hatch depends on the temperature. The warmer it is, the sooner the chemical processes inside the egg can take place and hatching can follow.

Heat makes liquids boil. When they boil, they turn into gas. Here, heat from a flame is boiling a flask of water. You can see clear bubbles of steam (which is water gas) rising from the bottom.

When water boils in a kettle, steam comes out of the spout. At first the steam is clear, but as it quickly cools to below boiling point (212°F) it condenses into a cloud of tiny droplets, as shown here.

The uses of heat

Humans first discovered how to make fire thousands of years ago. It was one of the greatest discoveries, because it enabled people to keep warm, to cook food so it could be more easily digested and preserved, to make pottery utensils, and to form metals into tools and weapons.

Today heat is used in these and many other ways. The most important use is to provide the modern world with energy. When fuels are burned, heat is released. This heat can be turned into other kinds of energy, such as electricity to light and heat homes and offices. Or it can be used in engines to drive cars, aircraft, trains, and other forms of transport.

A horse being shod was a common sight in the days before cars. This man is fitting a hot iron shoe onto the hoof of a horse. The shoe is so hot that it makes the hoof smoke. Earlier, he had heated the shoe until it was red-hot. Then he hammered it to fit the hoof.

Bonfires

Fire was very important to early people. Often it meant the difference between life and death for them in cold weather. Some old festivals survive at which bonfires are lit. People look forward again to the days of summer when the sun will heat the land.

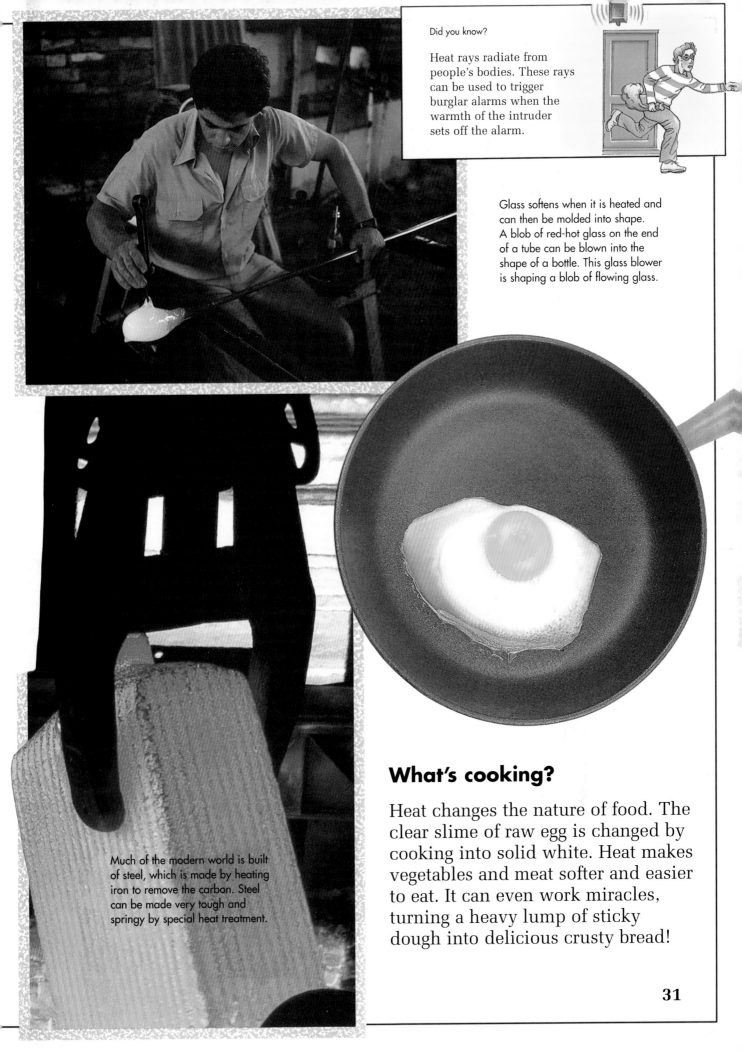

Glass softens when it is heated and can then be molded into shape. A blob of red-hot glass on the end of a tube can be blown into the shape of a bottle. This glass blower is shaping a blob of flowing glass.

Much of the modern world is built of steel, which is made by heating iron to remove the carbon. Steel can be made very tough and springy by special heat treatment.

What's cooking?

Heat changes the nature of food. The clear slime of raw egg is changed by cooking into solid white. Heat makes vegetables and meat softer and easier to eat. It can even work miracles, turning a heavy lump of sticky dough into delicious crusty bread!

31

Heat words

Ash Powdery, unburned chemicals left behind after something has been burned.

Bacteria Microscopic creatures.

Blubber Fat layer under the skin of some animals.

Carbon Substance found in all animals and plants. Coal is mainly carbon.

Cells All living things are made up of tiny units called cells. A human body contains millions.

Charcoal A form of carbon made by heating wood.

Chemical energy Energy contained in chemicals.

Condense To turn from a gas into a liquid.

Conduction Movement of heat through something. Heat is conducted from a hot drink through a teaspoon into your fingers.

Convection Movement of heat as a result of rising currents of air or water.

Crystals Solids with regular geometric shapes.

Electrical energy Energy in the form of electricity.

Electromagnetic waves Waves that travel through the air or through space. Heat, light, and radio are electromagnetic waves.

Energy Power or force needed to move something.

Evaporate To change from liquid or solid to a gas.

Fossil fuels Gas, oil, and coal.

Friction A force that tries to stop things sliding over each other.

Fungi Plants with no leaves, flowers, or green coloring. Mushrooms are fungi.

Geyser A natural hot spring that shoots water and steam into the air.

Insulation Material that slows the loss of heat.

Iron A metal, mined from the ground and used to make cast iron, steel etc.

Methane A colorless, odorless flammable gas that contains carbon.

Nuclear energy Energy obtained by splitting (or joining together) the tiny particles of which substances are made.

Oxyacetylene A mixture of the gases oxygen and acetylene, which burns with a very hot flame.

Radiate/Radiation To travel outwards in waves.

Vacuum An empty space, with the air removed.

Vapor A gas formed from something that is normally a liquid or a solid.

Weld To heat metals so they melt together.

Index

PICTURE CREDITS

All photographs are by Kim Taylor and Jane Burton except for those supplied by Eye Ubiquitous: *title page*, 6 *bottom*, 7 *top, inset* and *bottom*, 15 *top left* and *bottom*, 20 *bottom left*, 23 *bottom right*, 27 *center right*, 30 *top*; Tony Potter: 20–21 *center*, 30 *bottom*; Zefa: *cover*, 3, 5 *center*, 9 *top left*, 11 *top*, 12 *bottom*, 13 *bottom*, 14 *bottom left* and *right*, 21 *top right*, 24 *bottom left*, 26 *bottom*, 31 *top* and *bottom*.